ISSUES
today

36208

D1824270

Relationship Abuse

Edited by Christina Hughes

Series Editor: Cara Acred

Vol.113

Independence Educational Publishers

First published by Independence

The Studio, High Green, Great Shelford

Cambridge CB22 5EG

England

© Independence 2016

ISBN-13: 9781861687548

Acknowledgements

The publisher is grateful for permission to reproduce the material in this book. While every care has been taken to trace and acknowledge copyright, the publisher tenders its apology for any accidental infringement or where copyright has proved untraceable. The publisher would be pleased to come to a suitable arrangement in any such case with the rightful owner.

Illustrations

All illustrations, including the front cover, are by Don Hatcher.

Images

All images courtesy of iStock, except page 8 © Pixabay, page 9 © Images Money and page 20 © Iván Melenchón Serrano.

Icons on page 10 are made by Freepik from www.flaticon.com.

Editorial by Christina Hughes and layout by Jackie Staines, on behalf of Independence Educational Publishers.

Printed in Great Britain by Zenith Print Group.

Cara Acred

Cambridge

September 2016

Contents

About *ISSUES* today

ISSUES **today** is a series of resource books on contemporary social issues, designed for Key Stage 3 pupils and above. This series is also suitable for Scottish P7, S1 and S2 students.

Each volume contains information from a variety of sources, including government reports and statistics, newspaper and magazine articles, surveys and polls, academic research and literature from charities and lobby groups. The information has been tailored to an 11 to 14 age group; it has been rewritten and presented in a simple, straightforward and accessible format.

In addition, each *ISSUES* **today** title features handy tasks and assignments based on the information contained in the book, for use in class, for homework or as a revision aid.

ISSUES **today** can be used as a learning resource in a variety of Key Stage 3 subjects, including English, Science, History, Geography, PSHE, Citizenship, Sex and Relationships Education and Religious Education.

About this book

Relationship Abuse is Volume 113 in the *ISSUES* **today** series.

As many as one in five women accessing domestic abuse services have been experiencing abuse for more than ten years. Domestic abuse is not just physical, it can also include verbal, sexual, emotional and financial abuse. This book looks at abuse in all sorts of relationships: teenage relationships, elder abuse and even child-on-parent violence. It also addresses men suffering from domestic violence.

Relationship Abuse offers a useful overview of the many issues involved in this topic. However, at the end of each article is a URL for the relevant organisation's website, which can be visited by pupils who want to carry out further research.

Because the information in this book is gathered from a number of different sources, pupils should think about the origin of the text and critically evaluate the information that is presented. Does the source have a particular bias or agenda? Are you being presented with facts or opinions? Do you agree with the writer?

At the end of each chapter there are two pages of activities relating to the articles and issues raised in that chapter. The 'Brainstorm' questions can be done as a group or individually after reading the articles. This should prompt some ideas and lead on to further activities. Some suggestions for such activities are given under the headings 'Oral', 'Moral dilemmas', 'Research', 'Written' and 'Design' that follow the 'Brainstorm' questions.

For more information about *ISSUES* **today** and its sister series, *ISSUES* (for pupils aged 14 to 18), please visit the Independence website.

Intimate personal violence and partner abuse: statistics

Summary

This article presents findings from the year ending March 2015 Crime Survey for England and Wales (CSEW). It covers experience of emotional, financial and physical abuse by partners or family members, as well as sexual assaults and stalking by any person.

Main points

The CSEW estimates that 8.2% of women and 4.0% of men reported experiencing any type of domestic abuse in the last year. This is equivalent to an estimated 1.3 million female victims and 600,000 male victims.

There were 6.5% of women and 2.8% of men who reported having experienced any type of partner abuse in the last year, equivalent to an estimated 1.1 million female victims and 500,000 male victims.

Overall, 27.1% of women and 13.2% of men had experienced any domestic abuse since the age of 16, equivalent to an estimated 4.5 million female victims and 2.2 million male victims.

The decline in domestic abuse for all victims between the year ending March 2005 and the year ending March 2009 CSEW surveys was statistically significant. However, the current figure (6.1% for both men and women combined) continues a fairly stable trend seen since the year ending March 2009.

Women were more likely than men to have experienced intimate violence across all headline types of abuse asked about, for example, 2.7% of women and 0.7% of men had experienced some form of sexual assault (including attempts) in the last year.

Definitions of abuse in the intimate violence self-completion module

Intimate violence is the collective term used to describe domestic abuse, sexual assault and stalking. Categories used in the presentation of these statistics are defined as follows:

➢ **domestic abuse:** this category combines partner abuse (non-sexual), family abuse (non-sexual) and sexual assault or stalking carried out by a current or former partner or other family member – this broadly matches the Government's definition of domestic violence and abuse.

➢ **non-sexual abuse by a partner:** physical force, emotional or financial abuse or threats to hurt the respondent or someone close to them carried out by a current or former partner.

➢ **a non-sexual abuse by a family member:** physical force, emotional or financial abuse or threats to hurt the respondent or someone close to them carried out by a family member other than a partner (father/mother, step-father/mother or other relative).

➢ **sexual assault:** rape or assault by penetration including attempts ('serious'), indecent exposure or unwanted touching ('less serious') carried out by any person.

➢ **stalking:** two or more incidents (causing distress, fear or alarm) of receiving obscene or threatening unwanted letters, e-mails, text messages or phone calls, having had obscene or threatening information about them placed on the Internet, waiting or loitering around home or workplace, or following or watching by any person, including a partner or family member.

11 February 2016

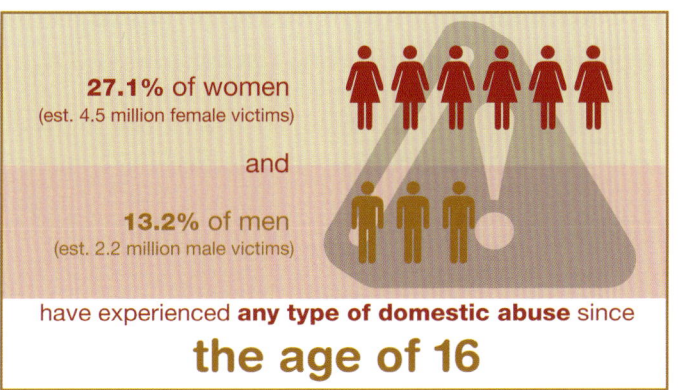

27.1% of women
(est. 4.5 million female victims)

and

13.2% of men
(est. 2.2 million male victims)

have experienced **any type of domestic abuse** since

the age of 16

www.ons.org.uk

Types of domestic abuse

There are many kinds of domestic abuse. Some of them are outlined here. Please be aware of what domestic abuse is and be sure you could recognise it in your partner's behaviour, your own behaviour or the behaviour of people you know.

Physical abuse includes:

➢ Hitting you
➢ Biting you
➢ Strangling you
➢ Kicking you.

Sexual abuse:

➢ Forcing you to have sex
➢ Touching you
➢ Making you do things you don't want to
➢ Not allowing you to take contraception
➢ Forcing you to look at or watch graphic materials.

Emotional or psychological abuse:

➢ Constantly checking up on you by phone or text
➢ Calling you names
➢ Putting you down
➢ Humiliating you
➢ Making you feel guilty or bad about yourself
➢ Threatening to take your children away
➢ Using your children to relay messages.

Financial abuse:

➢ Taking your money
➢ Taking your benefits
➢ Monitoring what you spend.

Social abuse:

➢ Stopping you from seeing your friends or family
➢ Stopping you from contacting your friends or family
➢ Checking your phone or text messages.

Forced marriage:

➢ One or both parties not wishing to be married
➢ Distinct from arranged marriage, where both parties have to agree to the arrangement of their marriage.

Honour-based violence:

➢ Extreme punishments or harassment for breaking a strict 'moral code'
➢ Fear of the above
➢ Punishment or harassment for supporting a victim of 'honour'-based violence.

Female genital mutilation:

(sometimes mistakenly called female circumcision)

May be seen by:

➢ Family belongs to a community in which female genital mutilation is practised and are making preparations for the child to take a holiday, arranging vaccinations or planning absence from school
➢ Prolonged absence from school with noticeable behaviour change on return, or
➢ Long periods away from classes or other normal activities, possibly with bladder or menstrual problems.

Socially isolating abuse:

➢ Not letting you go out or go out on your own
➢ Stopping you from seeing friends or family
➢ Stopping you from working
➢ Stopping you from having enough money to go out
➢ Stopping you from learning English.

www.lbbd.gov.uk

Domestic violence legislation in England and Wales

From curfews on wife beating to the creation of the first refuge: the landmark moments in the ongoing struggle to end domestic abuse.

1857 – Rule of Thumb
A judge reportedly states that a man may beat his wife so long as he uses "a rod not thicker than his thumb". Many people consider this to be common law throughout the 19th century.

1860 – Law of Coverture
At the point of marriage, a husband became legally responsible for the actions of both his wife and children. This meant he was entitled to use physical or verbal abuse to control their behaviour.

1870 – Married Women's Property Act
Before 1870, when a woman married, her property automatically became her husband's.
After this act, any money she earned or inherited while married stayed hers.

1895 – Curfew on wife beating
This city of London byelaw made hitting your wife between the hours of 10pm and 7am illegal – because the noise was keeping people awake.

1923 – Matrimonial Causes Act
This act marked a big change in divorce law. Before, a wife had to prove her husband had been unfaithful and show evidence of other faults. After 1923, adultery could be a sole reason for divorce for women as well as men.

1956 – Sexual Offences Act
This was the first time rape was defined under specific criteria, such as incest, sex with a girl under 16, no consent, use of drugs, anal sex and impersonation.

1971 – First safe house
The charity Refuge opens the first safe house in Chiswick, west London, for women and children fleeing domestic abuse.

1976 – Domestic Violence and Matrimonial Proceedings Act
This was the first legislation dedicated to combating domestic violence. It gave survivors new rights by offering civil protection orders (injunctions) for those at risk of abuse.

1977 – Housing Act (Homeless Persons) 1977
Women and children at risk of violence were acknowledged as homeless. This meant they gained the right to state-funded temporary accommodation.

1991 – Marital rape criminalised
Before 1991 it was a husband's legal right to rape his wife – marriage implied consent for sexual intercourse. This was the first time a woman had legal protection from marital rape.

2003 – Inter-ministerial group on domestic violence is established
This group received crucial evidence on the scale of domestic violence and use of refuges. Women's Aid (a charity dedicated to ending domestic violence) played a significant role in providing testimony.

2004 – Domestic Violence, Crime and Victims Act
This made common assault an arrestable offence. This meant that police could arrest a suspect immediately, rather than leaving them with someone vulnerable while they applied for a warrant.

2010 – Government strategy is set out to end violence against women and girls
The strategy developed a 2011 plan which included financial commitments to support rape crisis centres and specialist training for health workers in the treatment of survivors.

2014 – Clare's Law
A law is introduced across England and Wales which gives people the right to ask police about a partner's history of domestic abuse.

28 November 2014

The above information is reprinted with kind permission from The Guardian.
© 2016 Guardian News and Media Limited

www.theguardian.com

Abuse in teenage relationships

If you're in a relationship and you feel unhappy about or frightened by the way your partner treats you, you don't have to put up with it.

It can be hard to know what's 'normal' in a relationship. It can take time to get to know each other and discover what works for you both.

But there's one thing that's for sure: abusive or violent behaviour is not acceptable. If it's happening to you, it's OK to ask for help and advice.

Partner abuse can happen to anyone of any age, culture or religion. It can happen to boys or girls, but it's much more likely to happen to girls. Young people in same-sex relationships are also more likely to be affected.

Tink Palmer, a social worker who works with people who have been abused, says: "No-one should have to put up with violence in any form. If it's happening to you, talk to a person you trust, such as a parent, a trusted adult or a friend. Don't hold it in – talk to someone."

What is abuse in a relationship?

Abuse can involve physical violence, such as hitting, kicking, pushing, slapping or pressuring you into sex. But there are other forms of abuse, too.

Emotional and verbal abuse can involve your boyfriend or girlfriend:

➢ saying things that make you feel small, whether you're alone or in front of other people
➢ pressuring you to do things you don't want to do, including sexual things
➢ checking up on you all the time to find out where you are and who you're with – for example, texting or calling you a lot if you're out with your friends
➢ threatening to hurt you or someone close to you, including pets.

As well as happening when you're together, emotional and verbal abuse can happen on the phone or on the Internet.

Behaviour like this is not about love. It's about someone controlling you and making you behave how they want. People who abuse a partner verbally or emotionally may turn to violence later on in the relationship. This kind of controlling behaviour is a big warning sign.

Behaviour like this is not OK, even if some people tell you it is. Violence and abuse in relationships is not normal, it is not 'just the way things are' or 'messing around'. It's a serious issue.

Being hurt emotionally and physically can harm your self-esteem and make you feel anxious, depressed or ill. Young people who are abused can also develop eating disorders, problems with alcohol and drugs and be at risk of sexually transmitted infections and pregnancy from sexual abuse.

Getting help for abuse

If you're in a controlling or abusive relationship and you want help, don't be scared to talk to someone about it. Remember, it's not your fault, no matter what anyone says, and it is far better to talk about it with someone. It doesn't matter if you've been drinking or what you've been wearing. There is no excuse.

It can be difficult to find the right words to ask for help. Try asking someone whether you can talk to them about something. Tell them you need some help or that something is happening and you don't know what to do.

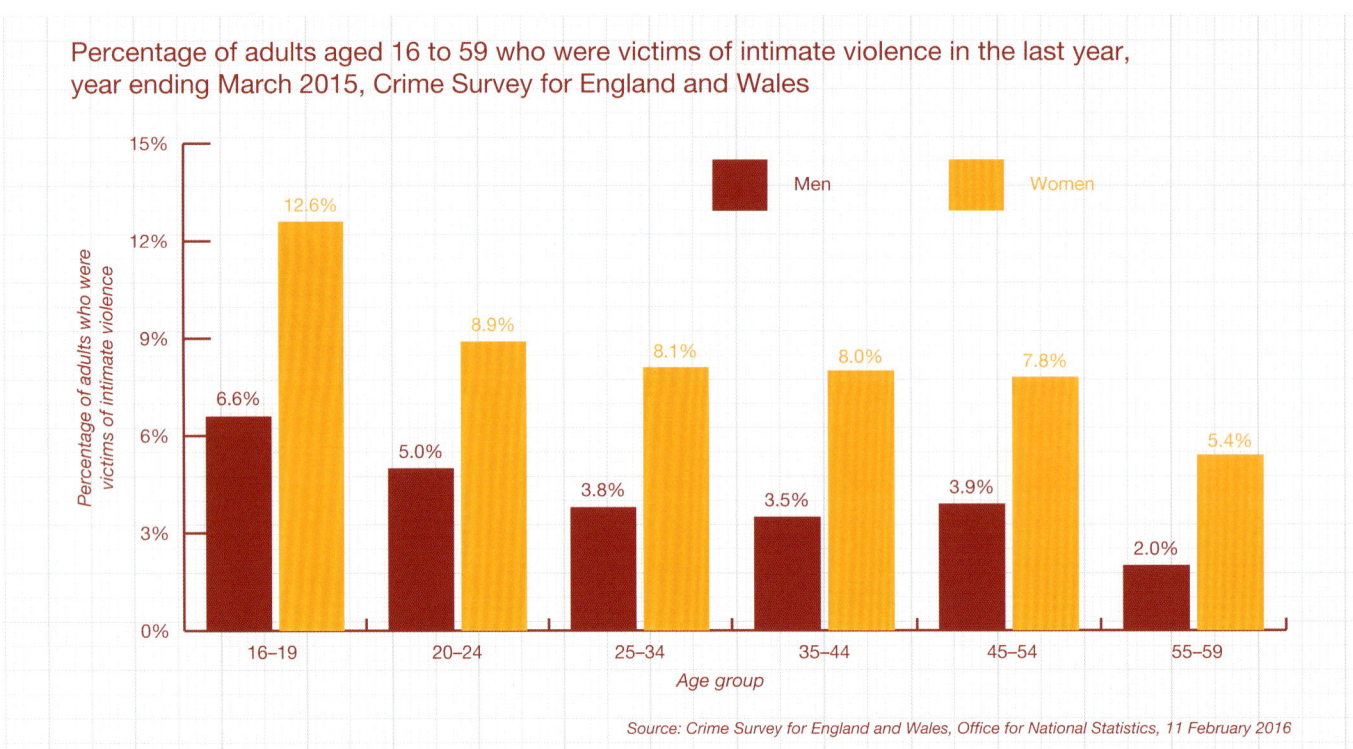

Percentage of adults aged 16 to 59 who were victims of intimate violence in the last year, year ending March 2015, Crime Survey for England and Wales

Percentage of adults who were victims of intimate violence

Men Women

Age group	Men	Women
16–19	6.6%	12.6%
20–24	5.0%	8.9%
25–34	3.8%	8.1%
35–44	3.5%	8.0%
45–54	3.9%	7.8%
55–59	2.0%	5.4%

Source: Crime Survey for England and Wales, Office for National Statistics, 11 February 2016

There are several people you might talk to, such as:

- an adult mentor or a favourite teacher at school
- your mum, dad or another trusted adult – perhaps a friend's mum
- an adviser on a helpline such as ChildLine (0800 1111)
- a GP or nurse
- a friend.

And remember, try again if you don't get the response you think you need. If you are in immediate danger, call 999.

If you think a friend is being abused

If you think a friend might be experiencing abuse, talk to them. "Keep calm, and don't be judgmental or condemning," says Palmer. "It can be difficult to talk to a friend, but try. If you're concerned, don't worry that you might be wrong, worry that you might be right."

Try asking your friend if you can talk about something. Tell them you're worried about them and ask them whether everything is OK. Listen to them and let them know that nobody has to put up with abuse.

If they have been hurt, offer to go to the doctor with them. Have the number of a useful helpline, such as ChildLine on 0800 1111, ready to give to them.

Your friend might be angry or upset with you for a while, but they will know you care and you might have helped them realise they can get help.

If you're abusing someone

If you're abusing your partner or you're worried that you might, you can call ChildLine on 0800 1111 or talk to a trusted adult.

"Recognising that your behaviour is wrong is the first step to stopping it. But you may need help to stop," says Palmer.

Sometimes the things that cause abusive behaviour, such as feelings about things that happened in the past, can be very powerful. "We can't always stop things on our own, or straight away," says Palmer. "We do need help, which is why it's important to talk to someone."

16 July 2014

> The above information is reprinted with kind permission from NHS Choices.
> © Crown copyright 2016

www.nhs.uk

Chilling film reminds us that older women suffer from domestic abuse, too

'Older women are often invisible in many spheres of life, and it can be all too easy to not see what is really going on.'

By Brogan Discoll

A powerful film is sending a chilling reminder that domestic abuse can happen to any woman, at any point in her lifetime.

Women's Aid has launched a new campaign 'Do You See Her?' to shine a light on the often invisible victims of domestic abuse: older women.

As many as one in five women accessing domestic abuse services have been experiencing abuse for more than ten years, the charity revealed.

One in four women will experience domestic abuse and two women in the UK are killed by a current or ex-partner every single week – and, frankly, we're at crisis point.

That's why Women's Aid has teamed up with Ridley Scott Productions to produce a short film about older women and domestic abuse.

The film, which stars Tessa Peake-Jones, tells the heartbreaking story of an older woman in an abusive relationship.

The film also stars Phil Davis as Peake-Jones' abusive husband and Anne-Marie Duff, as their daughter.

During the film Duff visits with the couple's young grandchildren for lunch. It is a comfortable, middle-class home – not the type of environment typically believed to be abusive.

Women's Aid has found in its 40 years of experience that older women often do not access support or ask for help, despite domestic abuse happening to women of all ages.

Peake-Jones, best known for her role in *Only Fools And Horses*, said: "I am proud to be raising awareness about domestic abuse affecting older women.

"Older women are often invisible in many spheres of life, and it can be all too easy to not see what is really going on.

"I want to give these women a voice: to show them that they are not alone, that they deserve help if they are experiencing domestic abuse."

Polly Neate, chief executive of Women's Aid, said in a statement: "The film is a stark reminder that even those closest to a woman who is being abused may not know what goes on behind closed doors.

"Any woman, of any age, can be forced to live in the invisible prison of domestic abuse – including those with adult children and grandchildren. Victim stereotypes are simply not relevant to our understanding of domestic abuse.

"We want to send a clear message to all older women experiencing abuse: Women's Aid is here for you. We will help you."

Speaking about the film, she added: "It has been a privilege to work with incredible actors and filmmakers to create this vital piece of work. Thank you all."

Director Paul Andrew Williams said: "Since learning more about the horrific, all-too common problem of domestic violence whilst working on *Murdered by my Boyfriend*, I felt that now, more than ever, we need to highlight the problem that many women face today.

"Whilst funding is being cut and important organisations are being forced to restrict the help they can offer vulnerable women, now is the time to raise awareness and show that there are people out there, like Women's Aid who can help."

7 June 2016

www.huffingtonpost.co.uk

#MaybeHeDoesntHitYou reminds us that domestic abuse is not just physical violence

By Brogan Driscoll

When people think of an abusive relationship, they often visualise cuts and bruises.

But domestic abuse is not just physical, it can include verbal, sexual, psychological, financial or emotional abuse.

Now, a hashtag is serving as a powerful reminder that a partner doesn't need to raise their fists to be abusive.

#MaybeHeDoesntHitYou tweets have been highlight the many, many ways a partner can be abusive:

➢ #MaybeHeDoesntHitYou but he makes sure you believe that you're too broken/damaged to ever be wanted by anyone else.

➢ #MaybeHeDoesntHitYou but instead he isolates you and destroys all of you platonic relationships so he's all you have.

➢ #MaybeHeDoesntHitYou but he compares you to other women, criticizes your body and constantly tells you, you aren't doing enough for him.

➢ #MaybeHeDoesntHitYou but he won't let you go home or see your friends very often or at all.

"The hashtag is a powerful reminder that domestic abuse is not just physical," Polly Neate, Chief Executive of Women's Aid, told The Huffington Post UK.

"Coercive control, financial abuse and emotional abuse are all part of domestic abuse – in fact, physical violence often comes later on in an abusive relationship.

"Coercive control – the insidious stripping away of a victim's self-esteem – is at the heart of domestic abuse. It's vital that this is understood by society as a whole."

Domestic abuse affects one woman in four at some point in her lifetime and it kills two women every week in the UK.

However, while the majority of victims are female and the majority of perpetrators are male, HuffPost UK acknowledge that victims can be male or female, as can perpetrators. This is why the following tweet is so important to remember.

➢ #MaybeSheDoesntHitYou is just as important as #MaybeHeDoesntHitYou because abuse doesn't care about your gender.

Useful contact numbers

Refuge – domestic violence help for women and children.

www.refuge.org.uk | 0808 2000 247

Women's Aid – support for abused women and children.

www.womensaid.org.uk

Or call the **National Domestic Violence Helpline**, run by Women's Aid and Refuge, on 0808 2000 247.

Broken Rainbow – the LGBT domestic violence charity.

www.brokenrainbow.org.uk | 0845 2 60 55 60

Men's Advice Line – advice and support for men experiencing domestic violence and abuse.

0808 801 0327

11 May 2016

My money, my life

Nearly one in five British adults say they have experienced financial abuse in an intimate relationship, according to a new campaign launched by the Co-operative Bank and Refuge, the national domestic violence charity.

The 'My money, my life' campaign raises awareness of the true scale of financial abuse for the first time, as it occurs within intimate relationships, where financial control, exploitation or sabotage are used to control a person's ability to acquire, use and maintain financial resources. The Co-operative Bank and Refuge carried out the UK's largest study to date in this area in order to understand the prevalence of financial abuse in intimate relationships in the UK. They are campaigning for the banking industry to come together to ensure there is proper support for the victims of financial abuse in relationships.

Key findings

➢ One in five UK adults is a victim of financial abuse in a relationship

➢ Half of victims experience a partner taking financial assets without permission

➢ For women, financial abuse rarely happens in isolation – 86 per cent experience other forms of abuse

➢ A third of financial abuse victims suffer in silence, telling no-one

➢ Six out of ten victims of financial abuse are women

➢ One in three people know somebody who has been financially abused.

The Co-operative Bank and Refuge are calling for industry-wide agreement to support people who experience financial abuse in their relationships.

What is financial abuse?

Financial abuse in intimate relationships is a way of controlling a person's ability to acquire, use and maintain their own money and financial resources.

Financial abuse is a form of domestic violence. According to financial abuse expert, Nicola Sharp-Jeffs from the Child and Woman Abuse Studies Unit (CWASU) at London Metropolitan University [it is best described as an example of intimate partner violence] domestic violence involves a pattern of behaviour that one person uses to control, undermine and obtain power over another person. Domestic abuse can include physical, sexual, psychological/emotional and financial abuse. More simply, financial abuse is a current

or former partner controlling someone's ability to acquire, use or maintain financial resources by preventing victims from earning or accessing their own money.

Examples include:

➢ Stealing money from a partner

➢ Preventing a partner from accessing their own/ joint account

➢ Damaging possessions which then have to be replaced

➢ Insisting benefits are in their name

➢ Putting debts in a partner's name

➢ Stopping a partner from going to work.

This abuse can also continue post-separation.

Lifting the lid on financial abuse
One in five UK adults is a victim of financial abuse in a relationship

The 'My money, my life' campaign seeks to establish, for the first time, the true scale of financial abuse as it occurs within intimate relationships in the UK. While other forms of domestic violence are well documented, the use of money to exercise power within a relationship is not yet fully recognised. Yet the impact of this form of abuse – where financial control, exploitation or sabotage are used to control a person's ability to acquire, use and maintain

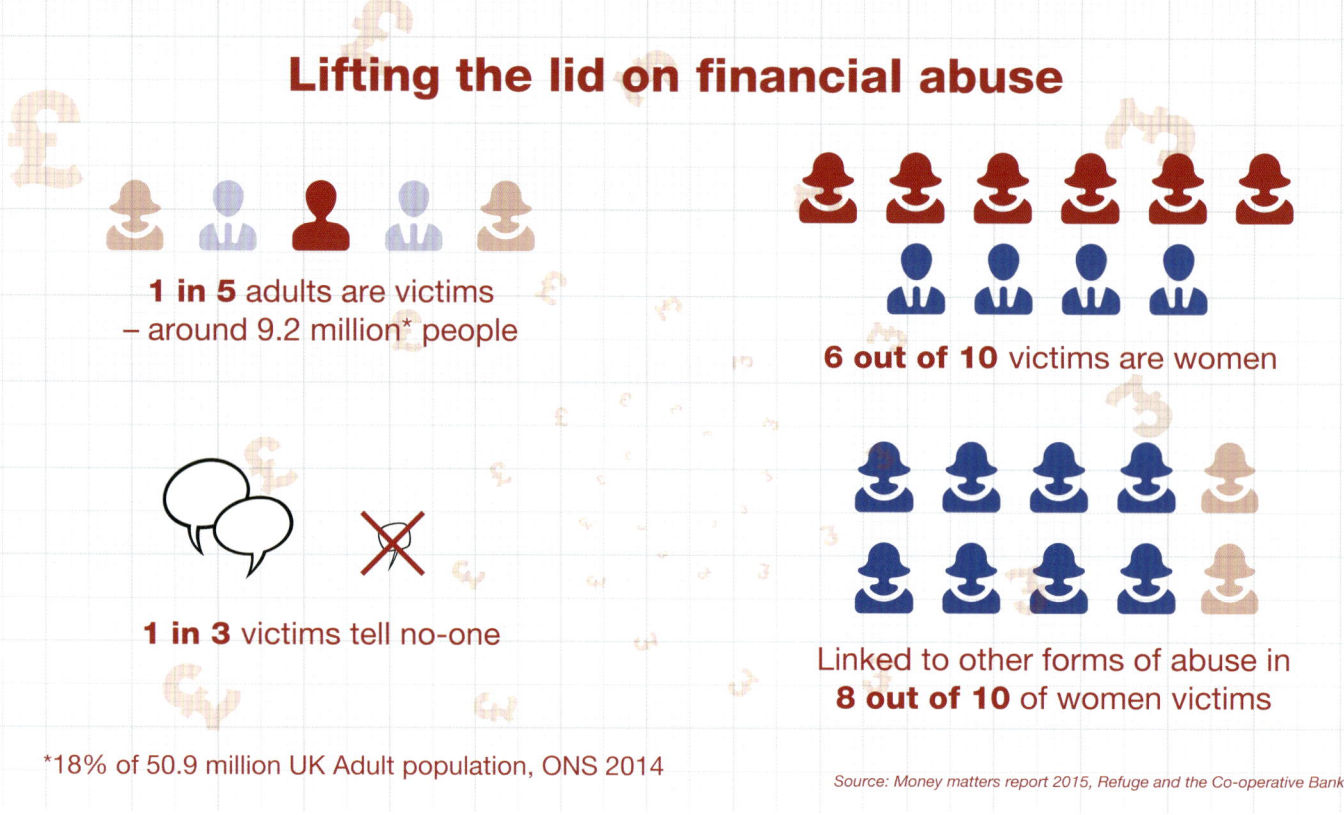

Lifting the lid on financial abuse

1 in 5 adults are victims – around 9.2 million* people

1 in 3 victims tell no-one

*18% of 50.9 million UK Adult population, ONS 2014

6 out of 10 victims are women

Linked to other forms of abuse in **8 out of 10** of women victims

Source: Money matters report 2015, Refuge and the Co-operative Bank

financial resources – can be both devastating and long-lasting.

This campaign launches with the publication of a new research report *Money Matters* – research into the extent and nature of financial abuse in relationships in the UK. The research report combines a study of over 4,000 adults with academic analysis and research interviews undertaken with 20 survivors of domestic abuse who had accessed Refuge's specialist services.

➢ Financial abuse against women is more likely to start at key life stage events compared to men, for example, when moving in with a partner, getting married or having a baby.

➢ Financial abuse in relationships against women also lasts for a longer period of time compared to men.

➢ Women are also more likely to experience financial abuse in multiple relationships and post-separation.

➢ Women experiencing financial abuse in relationships were more likely to be heterosexual and living as married, with the highest amount of financial abuse occurring amongst full-time working women and women working part-time.

As women are the most affected group, and the research shows they are the least likely to contact their bank for help, breaking down the barriers to enable a woman to access support from her bank is a key part of the campaign.

Overall, the report shows that while the majority of people experiencing this type of abuse are in heterosexual relationships, people in same-sex or bi-sexual relationships were more likely to be victims of financial abuse than the rest of the population. In addition, those with a disability were also more likely to be victims of financial abuse in an intimate relationship.

If you are experiencing domestic violence:

The Freephone 24-hour Domestic Violence Helpline, run in partnership by Refuge and Women's Aid, offers a 24-hour confidential helpline for women who are experiencing domestic violence. It provides emotional and practical support, including referrals to refuges and other local services: 0808 2000 247. You can also visit: www.1in4women.com.

www.refuge.org.uk

www.co-operativebank.co.uk

www.cwasu.org

False accusations preventing men from reporting domestic abuse, study finds

Male victims of domestic violence are reluctant to report the abuse they suffer for fear of being accused of violence themselves, according to new research by a Teesside University academic.

Dr Jessica McCarrick, a Senior Lecturer in Counselling Psychology and Chartered Psychologist, says that men are often arrested under false accusations and their reports of being a victim of domestic abuse are dismissed at first.

She is calling for more to be done to support male victims of intimate partner violence – encouraging men to report abuse and feel assured they will be taken seriously.

Dr McCarrick has carried out interviews with male victims who say that, as well as the trauma of domestic abuse, their negative experiences are further made worse within the criminal justice system by being treated like the guilty party or feeling dismissed by the police.

The number of women convicted of committing domestic abuse has more than quadrupled in the past ten years from 806 in 2004/05, to 3,735 in 2013/14.

Statistics show that an average of one third of domestic abuse victims are male.

One man, who did not want to be named, said he was arrested on three separate occasions following false counter allegations from his wife.

He said: "In the latest incident I made the initial complaint to police as my wife assaulted me. But when they arrived, they showed little concern and instead arrested me because my wife made a counter allegation. I certainly feel that more compassion and empathy needs to be shown towards male victims of domestic violence."

Dr McCarrick, who works within Teesside University's School of Social Sciences, Business & Law, says that this type of account is not at all uncommon.

"Within my research, the predominant experience is of men being arrested under false charges and their disclosures of being the victim are not taken seriously, despite having evidence.

"Men find it incredibly difficult to talk about their experiences of domestic violence because of the shame and emasculation they feel is associated with it. To find the courage to speak out, only to be accused of violence themselves, is incredibly disheartening and ultimately prevents countless men from reporting intimate partner violence."

Dr McCarrick is calling for more understanding of the emotional experiences of men and encouraging a more balanced, gender-informed perspective of domestic violence.

"When there was a positive experience of a police member, one who offered advice about support services

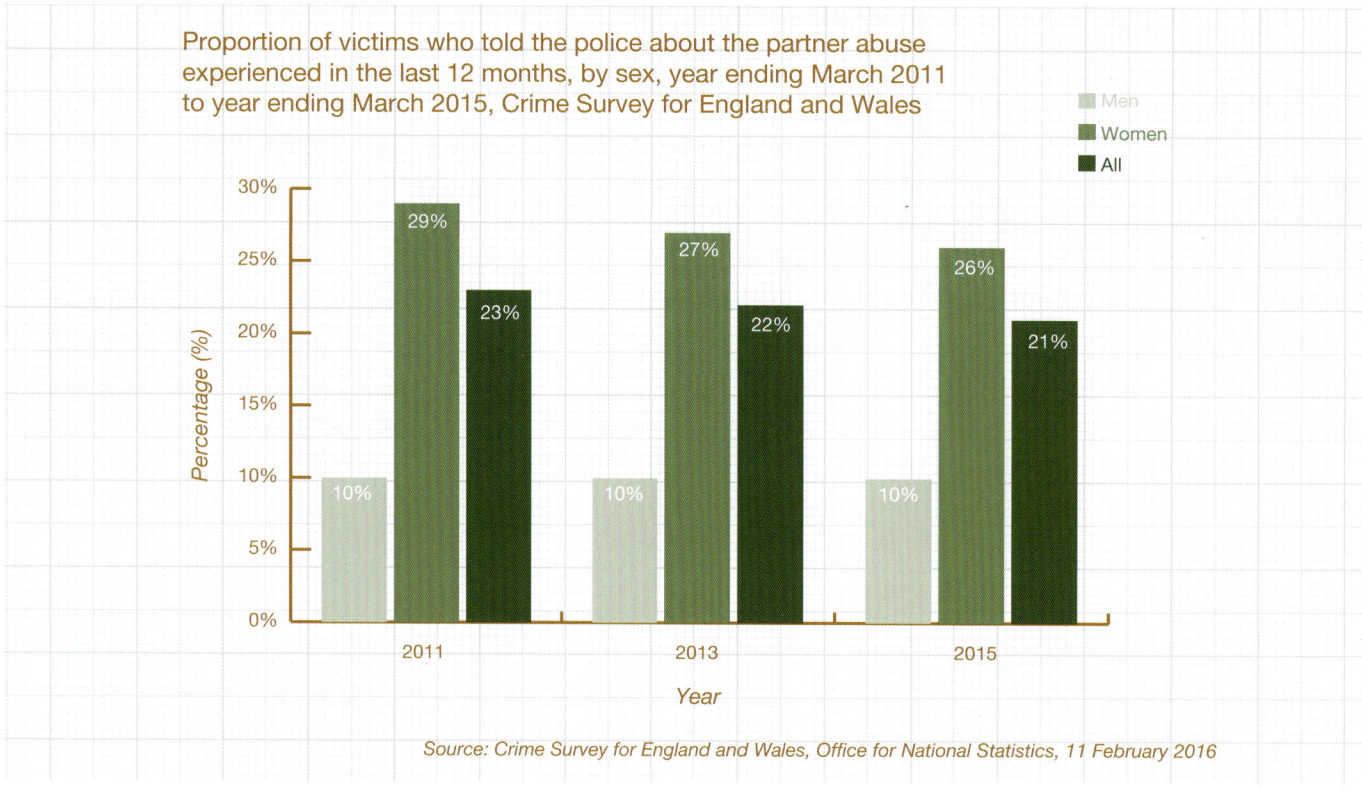

Proportion of victims who told the police about the partner abuse experienced in the last 12 months, by sex, year ending March 2011 to year ending March 2015, Crime Survey for England and Wales

Source: Crime Survey for England and Wales, Office for National Statistics, 11 February 2016

for example, this appeared to reduce the negative psychological impact of being arrested under false charges."

Intimate partner violence should be viewed as a human issue rather than a gender issue, argues Dr McCarrick and there should be more services and support to enable men to seek the help and sanctuary they desperately require.

She added: "Campaigners and researchers made waves in the 1970's, which had a positive impact and improved service provision for women – it is time to do the same for men.

"Promoting awareness of the plight of male survivors may encourage men to report abuse and feel assured that they will be taken seriously.

"Intimate partner violence is an issue which affects men and women within both heterosexual and homosexual relationships and I would like to see increased funding to improve service provision and development in order to support all people affected by this issue."

www.tees.ac.uk

Did you know?

Of those that suffered partner abuse in 2014/15, a higher proportion of men suffered from force (37%) than women (29%).

Male victims (29%) are over twice as likely than women (12%) to not tell anyone about the partner abuse they are suffering from.

The percentage of gay or bi-sexual men (6.2%) who suffered partner abuse in 2008/09 is nearly double the number for heterosexual men (3.3%).

One in every five victims of forced marriage is a man (20%). In 2013, 234 (18%) cases of forced marriage in the UK was where the victim was a man.

Source: Male victims of domestic and partner abuse 30 key facts, ManKind Initiative, March 2016

Mini glossary

Allegation – to accuse someone of doing something wrong or illegal, usually with little to no proof.

Emasculation – to be made to feel less masculine.

Exploitation – taking advantage of or using someone for selfish reasons.

Sabotage – to set up someone or something to fail on purpose.

What is elder abuse?

In 1993 Action on Elder Abuse (AEA) established the following definition of elder abuse. This has been adopted by the World Health Organisation, is promoted by the International Network for the Prevention of Elder Abuse and has been adopted by countries throughout the World, including the Republic of Ireland (with a slight addition):

'A single or repeated act or lack of appropriate action, occurring within any relationship where there is an expectation of trust, which causes harm or distress to an older person.'

It has at its heart the 'expectation of trust' that an older person may rightly establish with another person, but which is then violated. For this reason we do not involve ourselves with actions that relate to strangers, unless those strangers have abused the expectation of trust.

What happens and who is involved?

Any older person can potentially become a victim of elder abuse, which is why it is important to consider ways to self-protect. People can be abused in many different ways. There are five common types of abuse: physical, psychological, financial, sexual abuse and neglect. Often these abuses are also crimes.

We also have to recognise family abuse, which additionally manifests in the five types described above, but which can complicate the ability of an older person to accept or confront what is happening to them.

Abuse can occur anywhere

Both older men and women can be at risk of being abused, and this can potentially happen wherever they live or visit. This may include: someone's own home, in a carer's home, in a day centre, in a residential home, in a nursing home or in a hospital.

The key issue is not about where someone lives or visits, but about whether or not the opportunity exists for another to abuse the relationship of trust and exploit or harm them.

Which is why it is important to think in advance about ways in which someone can reduce the possibility of abuse, by avoiding isolation or dependency and by having more than one person keeping an eye on matters. Reliance on others does not mean having to be dependent on others. Thinking about self-protection is more about common sense than about being distrustful.

The victims

Both older men and women can be at risk of being abused. The Prevalence Study in 2007, which was undertaken following representations by AEA, indicated that 4% of older people (both men and women) experienced abuse in their own homes – at least 342,000 people. When this data was adjusted to include every instance of abuse the percentage figure rose to 8.6%

The abuser is often well known to the person being abused. They may be: a partner, child or relative, a friend or neighbour, a paid or volunteer care worker, a health or social worker or other professional. Older people may also be abused by a person they care for.

Understanding abuse

Often, the people who abuse older people are taking advantage of a special relationship. They are in a position of trust or have created an expectation of trust, whether through family bonds, friendship or through a paid caring role, and they exploit that trust.

In the experience of our helpline, most financial abuse is committed by family members, often sons and daughters, who will often seek to justify their actions, e.g. by claiming that they are taking their inheritance 'a bit early'.

Sometimes, however, abuse is not intentional. It can be because someone lacks the skills or external support necessary to adequately care for another person. We call this 'passive abuse' because it is unintentional. That does not mean that the impact on the older person is any less, but it can help us to understand how best to address the abuse.

www.elderabuse.org.uk

Pets caught up in domestic violence

It is becoming more and more common that family pets are used as a tool to manipulate and control victims of domestic violence. In addition, increasing research and clinical evidence suggests that there are inter-relationships, commonly referred to as 'links', between the abuse of children, vulnerable adults and animals. A better understanding of these links can help to protect victims, both human and animal, and promote their welfare.

The Links Group aims to raise awareness of the 'links' to all professionals in the hope that agencies will work together to help prevent related cases from going undetected.

Abuse to children, vulnerable adults or animals can have damaging and devastating effects for the victims, their families and wider society. If you are faced with this situation and don't know where to turn, you should know that there are organisations that can give you and your family safe refuge, whilst at the same time looking after the family pet.

It has been shown that:

➤ Where serious animal abuse has occurred in a household there may be an increased likelihood that some other form of family violence is also occurring.

➤ It is also apparent that children may be at increased risk of abuse in this environment.

➤ Acts of animal abuse may in some circumstances be used to pressure, control and intimidate a partner and children to remain in, or be silent about, their abusive situation. The threat or actual abuse of a pet can prevent victims from leaving situations of domestic violence.

An actual quote:

"He held my daughters' pets out of the upstairs window, and threatened to drop them if we did not return home."

In a survey by pet fostering charity Paws for Kids:

➤ 66% said their abuser had threatened to harm their pets

➤ 94% said if there had been a pet fostering service it would have made it easier for them to leave the violence, and so spare themselves and their children more abuse.

How it works

Petlink Raystede Home for Animal Welfare in East Sussex and part of The Links Group describe their procedure, "We take referrals from both agencies and/or directly from the owner, providing they can provide confirmation that they are fleeing domestic violence, i.e. an e-mail or letter from a case worker, the police or social services. We will then ask you to complete a variety of forms which include a pet information form and a legal contract. Once this information has been received we will endeavour to place your pet temporarily in a loving family home with a volunteer foster carer. Your pet will be reunited with you once you are settled and are able to have it back."

An actual story:

Joanna's domestic violence key worker contacted the Pet Fostering Service explaining she had been working with Joanna for the past six months, but Joanna would not leave her violent home until something could be sorted out for her two beloved dogs, Ruby and Toby. Referral forms were faxed and returned the same day. Arrangements were made to meet Joanna with Ruby and Toby the following day while she was on her way to the refuge. Obviously, she was very upset about parting with them, but knew it was the only way they would all be safe. Ruby and Toby jumped into the van and settled down together.

On arrival at the foster carer's house Ruby and Toby explored their new environment and within a couple of hours had made themselves quite at home, with Ruby on the sofa and Toby curled up on the rug in front of the fire. Joanna was offered a property within a few months and once she had settled in, was reunited her with her dogs.

www.pet-owners.co.uk

Activities

Brainstorm

1. What does the term 'domestic violence' mean?

2. There are many different types of domestic abuse. Can you list them?

Oral activities

3. With a partner look at the *Domestic violence legislation in England and Wales* on page 3 and discuss how the approach to domestic abuse has changed. Are there any particular landmark moments that surprise or shock you?

4. "The Prevalence Study in 2007, which was undertaken following representations by Action on Elder Abuse, indicated that 4% of older people (both men and women) experienced abuse in their own homes – at least 342,000." Discuss this statement in groups and talk about what elder abuse is, what happens, who is involved and how to spot the signs of elder abuse.

Research activities

5. Do some research and find out about male victims of domestic violence. Make notes on some of the statistics you discover and feedback to your class.

6. Not all domestic abuse is physical. Research the #MaybeHeDoesntHitYou and #MaybeSheDoesntHitYou hashtags and write up a summary of your findings.

Written activity

7. With a partner, create a five-minute PowerPoint presentation that explores the issue of domestic violence in teenage relationships. You should include a section about resources such as websites and charities that young people can consult if they are experiencing these issues.

Moral dilemma

8. As a class, discuss why you think male victims of domestic violence are less likely to come forward and talk about their abuse.

Design activity

9. Design a leaflet that could be displayed at your local vets, which offers advice for people who have pets and are concerned about what might happen to them if they were to leave their abusive partner.

One in three people do not know domestic abuse can happen after a relationship has ended

By Rachel Moss

You do not have to be in a relationship with a physically, emotionally or financially abusive person to be a victim of domestic abuse.

But new figures from Citizens Advice reveal that one in three people do not know that domestic abuse can happen between former partners.

The research also shows victims can be at greater risk of being harmed after leaving an abusive relationship, but many people are unaware that domestic abuse can continue when victims are no longer living with the perpetrator.

Our lack of knowledge may mean we're missing signs that suggest a friend or family member needs help.

The survey of over 2,000 British adults found that just one in five (22%) think it is always easy to tell what counts as domestic abuse.

A total of 13% believe domestic abuse can only be between two people in a relationship who live together, not among those who are casually dating.

Abuse that occurs after a relationship has ended often includes a financial or psychological element, but the report revealed that our knowledge in this area is seriously lacking.

Speaking to HuffPost UK Lifestyle, director of policy at Women's Aid Hilary Fisher said it is "deeply concerning that domestic abuse is not always recognised for what it is".

"It means that women are less likely to receive the support they need to move past their abuse. We need a huge cultural change around understanding what domestic violence is," she added.

Last year, the Citizens Advice report *Controlling Money, Controlling Lives* revealed that victims of financial abuse had access to their bank accounts

restricted, were stolen from and had their property destroyed.

Some victims sought help after being left with huge debts when they were forced to take out loans for their abuser. The financial abuse was in some cases accompanied by intimidation, physical violence and repeated death threats.

An analysis of almost 200 cases of financial abuse brought to local Citizens Advice between January and June last year [2014] revealed that nine in ten victims were women.

However, the new research showed that people are more than twice as likely to know that domestic abuse can include a psychological element than a financial one.

Only two in five (39%) are aware of the financial side of abuse compared to four in five (86%) who are aware of the psychological side.

On top of that, two in five people (39%) are not aware that making a partner account for all their spending can constitute domestic abuse.

"The suffering of domestic abuse victims is going undetected. Many people do not realise abuse can occur after a relationship has ended and be financial or psychological, as well as physical," Gillian Guy, chief executive of Citizens Advice, said in a statement.

"Without the knowledge and understanding of the extent of abuse it is difficult for family and friends to make sure people get the help they need.

"New measures from the Government to make coercive control illegal will ensure those found guilty of these crimes are punished. For this to truly help victims the public and authorities need support to identify abuse."

Citizens Advice is currently developing new guidance that will aim to better equip everyone, from friends and family through to professionals, to identify all forms of abuse and take the right steps to help victims get the support they need.

For support on domestic violence here in the UK, you can contact Women's Aid – support for abused women and children – or call the National Domestic Violence Helpline, run by Women's Aid and Refuge, on 0808 2000 247. Contact Broken Rainbow – the LGBT domestic violence charity – on 0845 2 60 55 60.

Proportion of offences recorded by the police in England and Wales which were flagged as domestic abuse related, selected offence groups, April to December 2015

Offence group	Percentage
All offences	11%
Violence against the person	33%
Sexual offences	12%
Miscellaneous crimes	9%
Public order offences	8%
Criminal damage and arson	7%

Legend: ■ All offences ■ Percentage (%)

Source: Crime in England and Wales: Year ending December 2015, Office for National Statistics, 21 April 2016

Or contact Men's Advice Line – advice and support for men experiencing domestic violence and abuse – on 0808 801 0327.

2 July 2015

www.huffingtonpost.co.uk

Mini glossary

Coercive – *to coerce someone means to force them into doing something.*

Perpetrator – *person who has committed a crime.*

NHS 'must do more' to protect domestic abuse victims

Too often the NHS is missing opportunities to stop domestic abuse, according to a damning report published on 25 February 2015 and shown to Channel 4 News.

The report, compiled by the domestic violence charity SafeLives, found that, on average, over 85 per cent of victims were in contact with A&E units, GPs or the police in the year before they finally got effective help to stop the abuse, writes Matthew Cundall.

The charity examined almost 5,500 domestic abuse cases, all of which occurred between 2013 and 2014.

Not every contact related specifically to domestic abuse, but they all presented opportunities, says the charity. It claims that if the health service was more proactive it could get support to many thousands of victims suffering in silence.

Rebecca Coombs was barely 21, a mother of two, when she was hospitalised for the first time by her partner. She was beaten so badly she was taken by ambulance to A&E. But no-one asked her, she claims, who had beaten her up.

Hospitalised

Eventually, when she was hospitalised for the third time, Rebecca pressed charges and she says she finally got the help she needed.

A recent report by Her Majesty's Inspectorate of Constabulary suggested that nearly half of all domestic abuse victims do not go to the police. It is why SafeLives wants to see much more of a lead coming from the health service.

When asked if the health service has made domestic violence a priority, the charity's Chief Executive Diana Barran told Channel 4 News: "No, they have not made it a priority.

"We think there are about 100,000 victims in this country, who have about 130,000 children in their homes, who are experiencing the most extreme abuse today, and about 250,000 who are suffering significant abuse; in our jargon we would describe them as medium risk.

Fear and violence

"Most of those medium risk are being missed today and nearly half of the high risk. So we could probably find another 300,000 people who are suffering fear, violence and coercion, if the health service was being really proactive.

"Although there's been lots of guidance and lots of good intention the actual execution from our perspective has been very limited."

Channel 4 News went to Bristol Royal Infirmary to see how it is training its frontline healthcare staff to better spot the signs of domestic abuse.

Specialists

Bristol is one of a number of hospitals which now has in-house specialist domestic violence advisers (IDVAs), like Punita Bassi. Her job is to spot victims when they present at A&E and act as a first point of contact.

And in the last four years since the scheme began, the response has been huge, they told us, with over a thousand victims of domestic abuse referred to a specialist by frontline staff.

Ms Bassi told us that before the advent of IDVAs, there were 11 domestic violence referrals in 11 months. In the same time period since, there have been 70.

But A&E Consultant Dr Rob Stafford, when asked what his message to the Department of Health is, said: "Domestic violence (DV) is a very important problem that we are starting to address and we have come a long way in addressing, but I think there is still room to improve in the way we detect DV and the way we approach its management."

24 February 2015

Things you can do if you're in an abusive relationship

Steps you can take to help keep yourself safe if you are in an abusive relationship.

There are things you can do to help keep yourself safe:

➢ Keep important phone numbers to hand for you and your children.

➢ Tell friends or neighbours about the abuse – ask them to call the police if they hear angry or violent noises.

➢ Practice ways to get out of your home quickly and safely.

➢ Keep safer places in your home where there are exits and no weapons.

If you are thinking about leaving your abusive partner, consider:

➢ who you will phone during a crisis

➢ agreeing a 'code word' you can use to indicate your fears to the police or other services

➢ keeping your mobile phone fully charged and topped up at all times

➢ identifying where you will make an emergency call if you don't have your mobile

➢ keeping the car filled up with petrol

➢ keeping spare car and home keys within easy reach or by your escape route

➢ rehearsing an escape route with children and teaching them how to phone the police

➢ where you will tell children to run to for safety during an attack

➢ identifying where and when you are most vulnerable to an attack

➢ planning how you can increase your safety at these times.

Keep an escape bag

Organise an escape bag which you can keep by your escape route or with someone you trust. It should include:

➢ passport

➢ birth certificate

➢ benefits book

➢ driving licence

➢ national insurance number.

Also, pack a change of clothes, snacks, spare money and a list of important phone numbers. Include items you feel you can't live without, such as your children's favourite toys, photos and keepsakes.

In an emergency always call the police on 999.

www.westsussex.gov.uk

British Muslim women's helpline: their voices won't go unheard again

Today [14 January 2015] sees the launch of the first national helpline for Muslim women and girls, tackling problems such as sexual abuse, forced marriage and divorce – still taboo subjects in their communities. Alia Waheed speaks to the people behind it.

By Alia Waheed

When the Muslim Women's Network (MWNUK) launched a report, last year, on sexual exploitation in the Asian community, it could only have dreamed that something like this would come to pass.

That report was called *Unheard Voices – The Sexual Exploitation of Asian Girls and Young Women.* Its publication coincided with the revelations around child sexual exploitation by Asian gangs in Rotherham and challenged the view that the issue was purely one of race and that somehow, Asian girls were left untouched by abusers because of loyalties to their own culture.

MWNUK found that a worrying number of women and girls were slipping through the net, as agencies – such as social services and the police – grappled with the difficulties reaching out to victims because of cultural sensitivities – those same points of faith which are exploited by their abusers to ensure their victims' silence.

It confirmed what many already knew – that many Muslim girls and women are trapped in a cycle of abuse and violence because of a lack of services. What's more, it recommended a helpline be set up as an outlet for them to confide their problems and seek advice.

And today, as a result of the charity's awareness-raising activities, the first national helpline for Muslim women is being launched by Minister for Women and Equalities, Jo Swinson.

The helpline will initially be run part time by trained, bilingual staff and will be accompanied by a website containing information on the issues which they are most commonly asked about: sexual abuse, domestic violence and divorce.

Its aim? To make sure the voices of Muslim girls and women never go unheard again.

Sadly, it's impossible to know just how many are suffering right now. Figures for violence against women in the Muslim community remain elusive.

Last year, the Home Office Forced Marriage Unit was informed of 1,302 cases. Of these, 15 per cent of victims were under 15, though figures peaked in the 16 to 17 age group, coinciding with the age that young women finish school. While the Iranian and Kurdish Women's Rights Organisation found, under the Freedom of Information Act, that more than 2,800 incidents of 'honour'-based violence were reported to police across the UK in 2010.

Within four months of its report last year, MWNUK had received 35 case studies from different agencies – a surprising number from what is traditionally such a closed community and especially considering the intimidation victims often face from their abusers, in the name of 'family honour'. It suggests that the real number is much higher.

Among them was a young woman, raped by 30 men, including a father and his schoolboy son, during a horrific six-hour attack. The common factor in each case? That cultural and religious issues were perpetuating the abuse and preventing victims from accessing help.

The desperate need for a helpline was cemented by the growing number of calls MWNUK staff were receiving from desperate women.

"We are predominantly a campaigning organisation but found we were getting many helpline-type enquiries," said Shaista Gohir MBE, Chair of MWNUK.

"These calls confirmed that there's definitely a gap in services for Muslim women, which are faith and culturally sensitive and non-judgemental. While there are services for specific issues such as domestic violence, there hasn't been a general helpline."

The charity also found many women were struggling to reconcile their faith with their problems. They simply couldn't find an alternative perspective to those patriarchal interpretations – which so often dominate religious discourse – that had been used against them.

"More women are asking about the religious implications of issues like abortion," explains Shaista "Often they feel that Islam cannot be as harsh as they've been led to believe. We can understand that predicament.

"We don't pretend to be religious scholars, or force our beliefs upon them. We give them a range of religious perspectives and show them that their faith does make allowances."

MWNUK began as an advisory group to the Government on issues relating to Muslim women and public policy in 2003, before becoming an independent organisation four years later.

The Birmingham-based charity now consists of a network of nearly 700 individuals and organisations, and has become one of the leading campaigning voices for Muslim women in the UK.

The power of that collective voice led to 19-year-old Shabana* contacting the charity after the attempted rape of her sister, then 11, by their uncle.

"Our dad left when we were small and mum had health problems so her family helped a lot," she explains. "But as we got older, we grew aware of how controlling my uncle was and how my mum and her sisters were scared of him. They had to ask for permission every time they went somewhere.

"Once I went with my grandmother to stay with cousins, while their mum was in hospital. When my uncle found out, he told my mum to bring me home or he would kill her and burn the house down."

It was while her grandmother was in Pakistan, that their uncle began bombarding Shabana with calls, trying to lure her to her gran's empty flat.

"He claimed he had pictures of me with boys and wanted to meet at the flat to discuss them, or he'd tell my mum.

"Every time he texted me to meet up I'd swear at him. But he'd always reply back that he loved me. I threatened to call the police, but he told me to go ahead because my mum wasn't going to believe me over him.

"I knew this was true, so I never told anyone."

A few weeks later, while Shabana was at a driving lesson, their uncle turned up at the family home and offered to take her 11-year-old sister shopping. Instead he took the terrified youngster to their grandmother's flat and tried to rape her.

"When I got home, she started crying and said 'it's uncle, he kissed me, touched me and made me do things'. I screamed the house down and phoned the police. Even then, my mum told me to stop so we could

> **DID YOU KNOW?**
>
> *Forced marriage is not a problem specific to one country or culture: since it was established in 2005, the Forced Marriage Unit (FMU) has handled cases relating to over 90 countries across Asia, the Middle East, Africa, Europe and North America.*
>
> *In 2015, the FMU handled cases involving 67 'focus' countries which a victim was at risk of, or had already, been taken to in connection with a forced marriage. The five highest volume countries in 2015 were:*
>
> - ➤ *Pakistan – 539 cases (44%).*
> - ➤ *Bangladesh – 89 cases (7%).*
> - ➤ *India – 75 cases (6%).*
> - ➤ *Somalia – 34 cases (3%).*
> - ➤ *Afghanistan – 21 cases (2%).*
>
> *In 2015, 175 (14%) of the cases handled by the FMU had no overseas element, with the forced marriage activity taking place entirely within the UK.*
>
> Source: Forced Marriage Unit Statistics 2015, GOV.UK, 8 March 2016

deal with it within the family. But I knew they just wanted to talk me out of it."

Shabana's uncle was arrested, but as the trial date got nearer, the pressure on her to withdraw the case grew.

"Our whole family was against us. They went on about family honour, playing the religious card to make us feel guilty and accused my sister of leading him on."

It was at this point that Shabana came across an article on MWNUK and contacted them. They were able to support the girls and raise awareness about their case.

"MWNUK understand about our culture and how, when things like this happen within Muslim families, the first reaction is to keep quiet and make sure nobody finds out. But the charity are completely against that. Knowing we weren't alone gave us the strength to carry on."

Their uncle pleaded guilty to assault and oral rape and was sentenced to 64 months in prison in June.

Shabana added: "A helpline is needed because many Muslim women don't have anybody to turn to. It's not talked about in our communities."

One of the most recent cases the MWNUK dealt with concerned a 17-year-old victim of forced marriage. Aisha* faced months of emotional and physical abuse by her parents before she was taken to Pakistan to wed her 30-year-old cousin, who she'd never even met.

"It started off with lectures about family honour, but then they started beating me with leather belts. They took away my phone, purse and Western clothes. I wasn't allowed to see my friends or go to the shop unaccompanied," she explained.

When Aisha arrived in Pakistan, she was warned that if she didn't play the role of the happy bride, she would die.

"With my dad, it wasn't about family honour, but his honour. He threatened to kill me if I didn't go through with it. I knew he meant it.

"On the wedding night, I told my husband that I didn't want to sleep with him, so he forced me. He raped me three or four times each night. Then, in the morning, I had to pretend I was happy.

"When I came back to England, my parents thought I was happy, so they let me have my phone back. When everyone was asleep, I looked up forced marriages and found MWNUK.

"I told them what had happened. They calmed me down and advised me. One night, I ran away with nothing. MWNUK helped me find accommodation, food and clothes. They also assisted me in getting a legal and Islamic divorce. It's changed my life."

With the launch of the first national helpline for Muslim women and girls helpline, voices of women such as Aisha and Shabana will no longer remain unheard. The charity hope that more will find the confidence to come forward and seek help.

Perhaps, finally, the veil of silence which has kept these problems hidden for so long, will finally be lifted.

*Names and identifying details have been changed to protect the women's identities.

The Muslim Women's Network Helpline can be contacted on 0800 999 5786 or you can visit their website: www.mwnhelpline.co.uk.

14 January 2015

www.telegraph.co.uk

Mini glossary

Bilingual – someone who can speak two different languages.

Elusive – difficult to find.

Grappled – fought/struggled with.

Patriarchal – a system controlled by men (the patriarch).

Perpetuating – to continue and build upon.

Reconcile – to settle something and restore it to a friendly state/relationship.

Why are there no refuges for male victims of domestic violence?

According to a 2005 study, 15% of women and 6% of men in Ireland suffer some form of domestic violence. Yet none of the shelters in the country provide beds for men:

"There is not one bed for men suffering from domestic violence," said Niamh Farrell of AMEN, the only domestic violence resource in Ireland for men.

"If there is no bed for men there is no bed for the children [with the men]," she said, explaining that fathers or guardians may not want to leave their children in the domestic situation.

"You can encourage them to look for help but in terms of housing, we can't do anything to help them with that because there is no refuge."

This is ridiculous. Abused men face the same problems as abused women. They need to find a safe place for themselves and sometimes their children. If no-one provides them with safe housing, many abused men end up in homeless shelters and on the streets. This proves risky because some shelters will not accept men with children, and obviously living on the streets with a child is a poor option. That leaves two options: remain in the abusive situation or leave the situation yourself, but leave the children with the abuser.

Both are unthinkable, yet little is done to help abused men seeking shelter. Many abused men assume that they have access to equal services:

"[They] will ring and assume that there are the same services for men and women, they ask 'where do I go?', 'but there's one for women, there should be one for men'. They just think there should be same services for men as there are for women."

There should be. There is no excuse for not providing men with the same support given to women. The argument that women are in greater need of help falls flat. The majority of victims of violence are male, yet no hospital turns away women because they see more men.

This is not how one runs a support service. One should provide access for everyone because one never knows when it is needed. It is particularly important in this situation because so few abused men come forward. Perhaps we will find that there are more abused men than we think if we open the doors to them.

7 July 2014

Disclaimer: This is a commentary based on an article originally published on Yahoo! News UK. The original article can be found at https://uk.news.yahoo.com/why-no-refuges-male-victims-domestic-violence-075147102.html#Ru7JruX

The above information is reprinted with kind permission from Toy Soldiers.
© Toy Soldiers 2016

toysoldier.wordpress.com

Helping parents suffering at the hands of children

In 2014, West Midlands Police dealt with more than 17,000 domestic abuse related crimes.

Among those who turned to the force's specialist Public Protection Unit for help breaking free from behind-closed-doors abuse was a woman who'd been assaulted – kicked, punched, throttled and spat at – on an almost daily basis.

It was an awful catalogue of abuse stretching back several years. And even more shocking when she disclosed the offender was not a violent partner… but her 12-year-old daughter.

Child-on-parent abuse was thrust into the spotlight this summer courtesy of a *Coronation Street* storyline in which Leanne Battersby suffered at the hands of her 12-year-old stepson Simon.

What started with sullen stares quickly escalated to unruly behaviour, verbal abuse and, ultimately, physical assaults … and left Leanne toying over how to deal with the tearaway and whether to call in outside help.

But such episodes aren't just soap opera fiction.

It's estimated that one in ten parents have experienced violent outbursts from a child, while national helplines are taking around 11,000 calls a year from parents being abused and seeking support to control children.

Between April '14 and March '15, West Midlands Police received 460 reports of under-18s committing domestic offences. Of those, 194 were child-on-parent offences, including 115 physical assaults, plus threats to kill, criminal damage, domestic thefts and fraud.

The youngest offender was a 12-year-old girl from Coventry whose mum called police to report being at breaking point following repeated attacks that started when her daughter was aged just eight.

She was arrested on suspicion of assault in January this year but, following enquiries by Public Protection officers who are specially trained to deal sensitively with such cases, the woman chose not to make a complaint and the case was filed.

The case is now managed by children's services; the girl is being supported by child mental health specialists (CAMHS) to manage anger issues, while other children in the family have allocated social workers.

Public Protection Inspector Sally Simpson said: "Incidents range from humiliating language and threats, belittling a parent and damage to property, to stealing from the home or bouts of explosive violence. And the outbursts, usually in the home, can be sparked by the smallest of incidents.

"Around six in ten such allegations passed to us are dropped because the victim decides not to support a formal prosecution. Understandably, most are reluctant to criminalise their own children and will exhaust all other options to address the issue, and try to change their child's behaviour, before resorting to a formal prosecution.

"They are challenging cases to investigate … and with repeat offenders the focus has to be on repairing a fractured family. We have to ask whether taking a child to court or blighting them with a police caution is in their best interests and will address underlying issues. Probably not … and if anything it can make matters worse."

Of the 194 under-18 child-on-parent crime reports received by West Midlands Police last year only 13 progressed to a formal charge, ten teenagers were given youth cautions and 12 complaints were dealt with through community resolutions.

Detective Inspector (DI) Simpson, added: "We've come a long way in just a few years because previously there may have been a temptation to lock a young offender in a police cell to 'teach them a lesson'.

"We do still get parents calling us in the hope police presence will act as a warning shot – and in some cases it helps – but we now have a holistic approach that involves working with agencies like child mental health (CAMHS) and education providers. Aggressive and conforming behaviours are learnt so working with partners to change mind-sets and behaviours is essential.

"Each case is different – but if there are genuine concerns for the parents' safety we would intervene and remove the child. It's always a balancing act."

Other recent cases dealt with by the force's Public Protection Units include a Birmingham mum punched in the face by her 15-year-old son when she asked him to help around the house, and a 15-year-old from Wolverhampton who hurled an ashtray through a TV screen during an argument.

Neither parent wanted police to pursue a criminal investigation – but DI Simpson said it's important domestic abuse sufferers contact police for support and guidance rather than suffer in silence.

She added: "Statistics show we've recorded almost 200 under-18 child-on-parent domestic crimes in 12 months … but I don't think there's any doubt it's an under-reported offence and I suspect the actual figure is much higher.

"Survivors tell us they'd been reluctant to contact police out of embarrassment, a feeling it would be admitting failing as a parent or a general unconditional love for their children. And sometimes there may be autism or other behavioural issues triggering outbursts that need to be taken into account.

"Another question parents are left asking themselves is how much rebelliousness they are expected to take as part of the growing-up process. This is purely subjective – but if lashing out at parental restrictions, or losing sight of boundaries, manifests itself in repeated aggression then I'd encourage parents to contact us.

"In the short term we can protect people and property. But we can also start the process with children's services, education, mental health or probation to ensure we have a clear understanding of the family history and develop a plan to best address a child's behaviour."

West Midlands Police recently doubled the number of officers in its Public Protection Unit – meaning one in ten of all officers now work in these specialist teams – and now has dedicated domestic abuse teams to investigate crimes, protect victims and manage offenders.

Detective Superintendent Angie Whitaker, force lead for domestic abuse, said: "A report by HMIC in March found West Midlands Police provides a good service when identifying and tackling domestic abuse – commending our investment in this area and the positive shift of culture across the force.

"These specialist units have all the knowledge and tactics they need to protect people from harm and I would urge all domestic abuse victims to speak out; they will be listened to, taken seriously and their report will be investigated fully."

To speak to your local Public Protection Unit call West Midlands Police on 101. More support is available through:

➢ www.youngminds.org.uk – a child mental health charity and parent helpline
➢ www.rosalieryriefoundation.org.uk – behavioural management specialising in domestic abuse and destructive relationships within families

2 October 2015

www.west-midlands.police.uk

Mini glossary

Holistic approach *– this refers to taking a more emotional and spiritual approach to something. For example, trying to engage and help the whole person in both a physical and mental manner.*

Subjective *– depends on the point of view. An idea that is shaped by a person's own personal experience or beliefs rather than pure fact.*

Domestic Violence Disclosure Scheme

Are you worried that your partner may have been abusive or violent in the past? The Domestic Violence Disclosure Scheme (DVDS) could offer more information about them if you have genuine concerns.

What is it?

The DVDS, often referred to as Clare's Law, gives men and women the power to ask whether their partner has a history of abuse and enables police to inform a potential victim of a partner's history in an effort to prevent them from coming to harm.

How can it help?

If police checks show that your partner has a record of violent behaviour, or there is other information to indicate that you may be at risk from your partner, the police will consider sharing this information with you.

The scheme aims to help you to make a more informed decision on whether to continue a relationship, and provides further help and support to assist you when making that choice.

Who can ask for a disclosure?

A disclosure under the scheme is the sharing of specific information about your partner with either you or a third person for the purposes of protecting you or another person from domestic violence.

- You can make an application about your partner if you have a concern that they may harm you.
- Any concerned third party, such as a parent, neighbour or friend can also make an application if they are concerned.

However, a third party making an application would not necessarily receive the information about your partner. It may be more appropriate for someone else to receive the information, such as you or a person who is in a position to protect you from the abuse.

How do I request a disclosure?

You can either:

- Visit a police station
- Call 101
- Speak to a police officer on the street.

Always dial 999 if there is an immediate risk of harm to someone or it is an emergency.

What can I do with the information?

The person receiving the disclosure can use the information to keep themselves and others safe, ask what advice and support is available and find out who they or others at risk should contact.

You may receive a disclosure even if you have not asked for one because the police receive information about your partner which they consider puts you at risk of harm from domestic violence. They may consider disclosing the information to you or another person who they consider best placed to protect you.

Police checks or any disclosures made are not a guarantee of safety but will ensure you are aware of local and national support available to you.

If you receive a disclosure it should be treated as confidential and it is only being given to you so that you can take steps to protect yourself or the potential victim. You must not share this information with anyone else unless you have spoken to the police, or the person who gave you the information, and they have agreed that it will be shared. The police may take action against you if the information is disclosed without their consent, which could include civil or criminal proceedings.

www.west-midlands.police.uk

Activities

Brainstorm

1. What is a refuge?

2. What is the Domestic Violence Disclosure Scheme (DVDS)? How does it work?

Oral activity

3. In pairs, discuss why victims choose to stay with abusive partners.

Research activity

4. Create a questionnaire to find out how many people in your class are aware that domestic abuse can happen after a relationship has ended. Use your findings to draw a graph that illustrates the results.

Written activities

5. Write a diary entry from the point of view of a domestic abuse victim. How do you feel? How might you handle this situation?

6. Read *British Muslim women's helpline: their voices won't go unheard again* on page 20. Write a summary for your local newspaper.

Moral dilemma

7. Your friend Saba has confided in you that her parents are planning to take her back to her home country and intend to marry her to her much older cousin who she has never met before. What do you do?

Design activities

8. Imagine you have been asked to design a leaflet that will be made available in your local GP's surgery. The leaflet should explain the key facts about domestic and relationship abuse, as well as busting some of the myths surrounding it. Include a list of resources people can go to for information and support.

9. Read *Helping parents suffering at the hands of children* on page 24. Create an informative poster surrounding the issue of child-on-parent abuse to help promote awareness.

Key facts

- The March 2015 Crime Survey for England and Wales (CSEW) estimates that 8.2% of women and 4.0% of men reported experiencing any type of domestic abuse in the last year (2014/15). This is equivalent to an estimated 1.3 million female victims and 600,000 male victims. (page 1)

- Female genital mutilation (FGM), sometimes mistakenly called female circumcision, is a form of domestic abuse. (page 2)

- Rule of Thumb: In 1857 a judge reportedly stated that a man may beat his wife so long as he uses "a rod not thicker than his thumb". Many people consider this to be common law throughout the 19th century. (page 3)

- In 2014, Clare's Law was introduced across England and Wales which gives people the right to ask police about a partner's history of domestic abuse. (page 4)

- Women's Aid has found in its 40 years of experience that older women often do not access support or ask for help, despite domestic abuse happening to women of all ages. (page 7)

- Domestic abuse affects one woman in four at some point in her lifetime and it kills two women every week in the UK. (page 8)

- Nearly one in five British adults say they have experienced financial abuse in an intimate relationship. (page 9)

- Men are often arrested under false accusations and their reports of being a victim of domestic abuse are dismissed at first. (page 11)

- The number of women convicted of committing domestic abuse has more than quadrupled in the past ten years from 806 in 2004/05, to 3,735 in 2013/14. (page 11)

- Of those that suffered partner abuse in 2014/15, a higher proportion of men suffered from force (37%) than women (29%). (page 12)

- The Prevalence Study in 2007 indicated that 4% of older people (both men and women) experienced abuse in their own homes – at least 342,000 people. (page 13)

- In a survey by pet fostering charity Paws for Kids, 94% said if there had been a pet fostering service it would have made it easier for them to leave the violence, and so spare themselves and their children more abuse. (page 14)

- One in three people do not know domestic abuse can happen after a relationship has ended. (page 16)

- In 2015, 175 (14%) of the cases handled by the Forced Marriage Unit had no overseas element, with the forced marriage activity taking place entirely within the UK. (page 21)

- It's estimated that one in ten parents have experienced violent outbursts from a child, while national helplines are taking around 11,000 calls a year from parents being abused and seeking support to control children. (page 24)

Glossary

Domestic abuse – Any incident of physical, sexual, emotional or financial abuse that takes place within an intimate partner relationship. Domestic abuse can be committed by a partner or family member and occurs regardless of gender, sex, race, class or religion.

Domestic Violence Disclosure Scheme (DVDS) – The DVDS, often referred to as Clare's Law, gives men and women the 'right to ask' police whether their partner has a history of abuse. The Police will carry out checks and, if they are at risk, can inform a potential victim of a partner's history in an effort to prevent them from coming to harm.

Elder abuse – Elderly people are vulnerable members of society and are at risk of abuse. For example, the abuser may be a neglectful caregiver or someone who takes advantage of their special relationship with an elderly person by exploiting them financially.

Emotional abuse – Emotional abuse refers to a victim being verbally attacked, criticised and put down. In order to gain control the abuser destroys a victim's self-esteem and mental wellbeing. A victim way also have been convinced by their abuser that the abuse is their fault. The abuser can use these feelings to manipulate the victim.

Financial abuse – Financial, or economic, abuse involves controlling the victim's finances. This limits the victim's independence and ability to access help, and restricts their ability to leave the abusive relationship. Financial abuse can include withholding money or credit cards, making the victim account for every single penny spent and forcing someone to quit their job or work against their will.

Forced marriage – A marriage that takes place without the consent of one or both parties. Forced marriage is not the same as arranged marriage, which is organised by family or friends but which both parties freely enter into.

Honour crime – An 'honour' crime or killing occurs when family members take action against a relative who is thought to have brought shame on the family. The victims are mostly women who are accused of dishonouring their family by going against their wishes (for example, by fleeing a forced marriage).

Physical abuse – Physical abuse involves the use of violence or force against a victim and can include hitting, slapping, kicking, pushing, strangling or other forms of violence. Physical assault is a crime and the police have the power to protect victims, but in a domestic violence situation it can sometimes take a long time for the violence to come to light. Some victims are too afraid to go to the police, believe they can change the abuser (who they may still love) or think their abusive situation is normal and do not realise they can get help.

Refuge – A shelter or safe house, offering a safe place for victims of domestic violence and their children to stay. Refuges can provide advice as well as emotional support for victims of domestic abuse until they can find somewhere more permanent to stay.

Sexual abuse – Sexual abuse occurs when a victim is forced into a sexual act against their will, through violence or intimidation. This can include rape. Sexual abuse is always a crime, no matter what the relationship is between the victim and abuser.

Stalking – Repeatedly following, watching or harassing someone. Stalking usually takes place over a long period of time and is made up of lots of different actions, some of which may seem harmless but which can be extremely distressing to the victim.

Verbal abuse – Spoken words out loud intended to cause harm, such as suggestive remarks, jokes or name calling.